KINGDOMS AND EMPIRES

The Rise, Fall, and Rescue of the Jewish Nation

First published in the United States of America in 1995 by Thomas Nelson, Inc., Publishers, Nashville, Tennessee, and distributed in Canada by Word Communications, Ltd., Richmond, British Columbia.

Text by John Drane

The author asserts the moral right
to be identified as the author of this work.

Published by
Lion Publishing plc
Sandy Lane West, Oxford, England
ISBN 0-7459-2173-6
Albatross Books Pty. Ltd.
PO Box 320, Sutherland, NSW 2232, Australia
ISBN 0-7324-0543-2

First edition 1995

10 9 8 7 6 5 4 3 2 1 0

Contributors to this volume
John Drane is Director of the Centre for the Study of Christianity and Contemporary Society at the University of Stirling and the author of several highly acclaimed books on the Bible and its background. In this book he presents the Bible and its history in a way that young people can understand and enjoy.

Alan Millard, Rankin Professor of Hebrew and Ancient Semitic Languages at Liverpool University, is the consultant for the illustrations in this book, and all the books in the series.

Acknowledgments
All photographs are copyright © Lion Publishing, except the following:
Robert Harding: 1 (left), 15 (left)
Z. Radovan, Jerusalem: 5 (middle), 14 (right)
Trustees of the British Museum: 9 (left), 15 (left)
Zefa: 13 (left)

The following Lion Publishing photographs appear by courtesy of:
The Biblical Resources Pilgrim Center, Tantur: 7 (left)
The British Museum: 5 (left), 6 (left, near right, far right), 8 (left), 11 (left and right), 16 (left), 17 (left), 20 (right)

Illustrations, copyright © Lion Publishing, by:
Chris Molan: 1, 2, 3, 4, 5, 6, 7, 8, 9, 10, 11, 12, 13, 14, 15, 16, 17, 18, 19, 20
Jeffrey Burn: 3 (left), 10 (right)

Maps, copyright © Lion Publishing, by:
Oxford Illustrators Ltd.: 2, 6, 11, 16, 19

Bible quotations are taken from the Good News Bible, copyright © American Bible Society, New York, 1966, 1971, and 4th edition 1976, published by the Bible Societies/HarperCollins. Used by permission.

Story text is based on material from *The Lion Children's Bible*, by Pat Alexander.

ISBN 0-7852-7907-5

Printed and bound in Malaysia

B·I·B·L·E WORLD

KINGDOMS AND EMPIRES

THE RISE, FALL, AND RESCUE OF THE JEWISH NATION

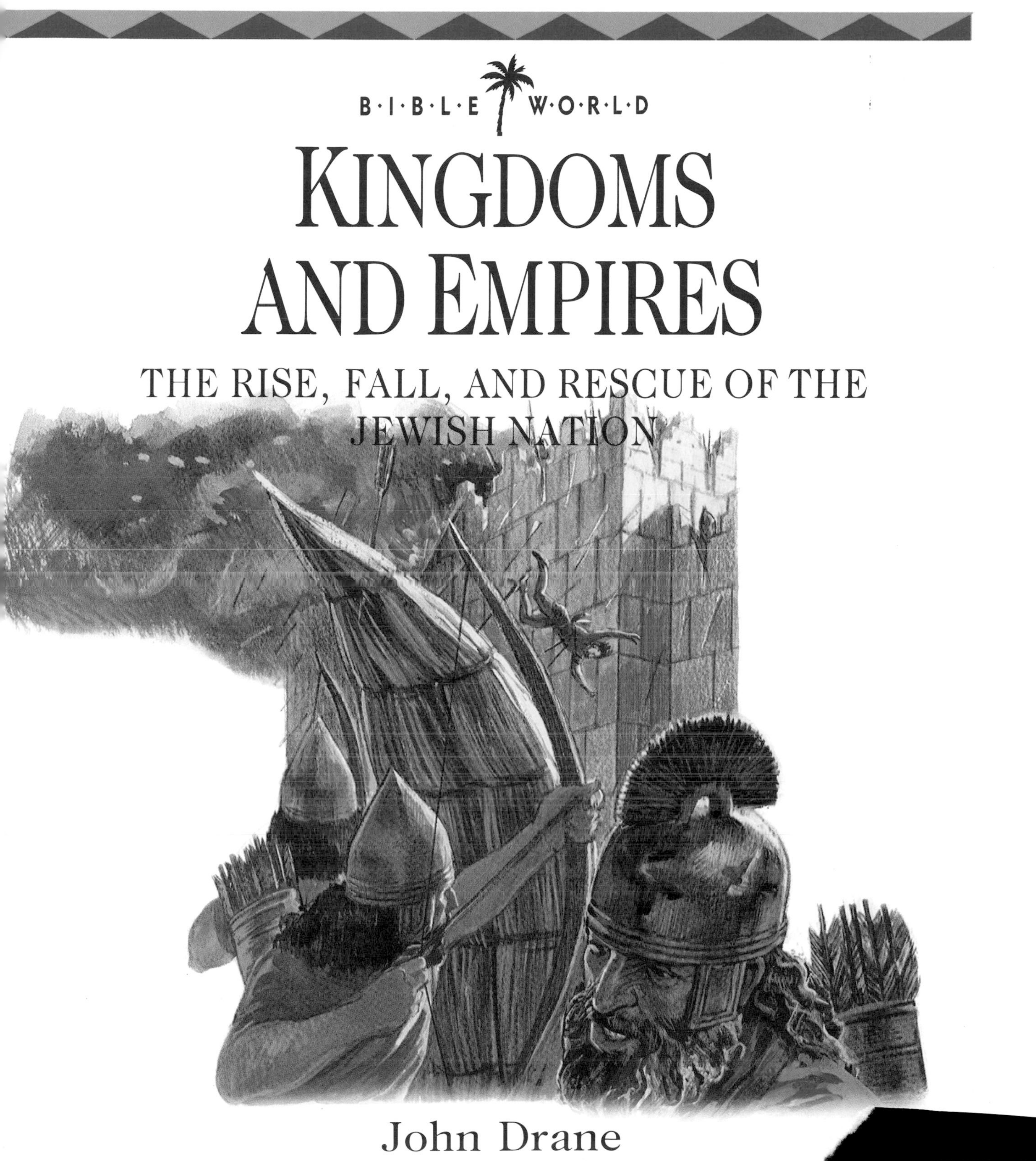

John Drane

THOMAS NELSON PUBLISHERS
Nashville · Atlanta · London · Vancouver

Contents

page 16

page 2

page 7

page 14

page 20

page 3

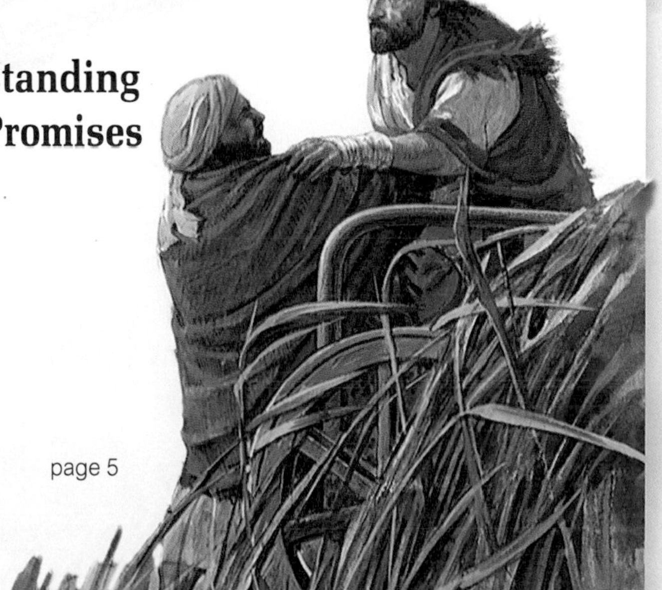

page 5

page 20

1 Solomon's Kingdom

The reign of King Solomon was a high point in the history of the people of Israel. After years of struggle against their enemies, they were able to live in peace.

They became wealthier, too. Solomon used some of the nation's riches to put up new and beautiful buildings in the capital city, Jerusalem. The greatest of these was the temple, which contained the covenant box with the laws God had given through Moses to their ancestors.

▲ Gold galore
The walls of King Solomon's temple were lined with gold rather like this Egyptian shrine.

Riches and poverty

Some people became very rich during the time of King Solomon, especially those who lived in Jerusalem. But most of the people lived in smaller towns and villages farther to the north. Unlike Solomon and his rich friends, they had to struggle to make a living. They were forced to pay more taxes all the time, and some of them even had to work for no pay on Solomon's great building projects.

Solomon's wrong turn

Solomon wanted to make his nation great. But he had forgotten lessons learned by his people long ago.

Once, Israel's ancestors had been slaves in Egypt: poor and powerless. With God's help, Moses had helped them escape from slavery and had taken them to a new land. This land had been shared among everyone, and everyone's share was equal.

Now Solomon was trying to change things, allowing some people to become rich while others grew poorer. The people became angry at the unfairness of it all, especially those who were not getting rich. A man named Jeroboam began a protest movement, supported by the people who lived in the poorer part of the country, the north. When King Solomon died, they saw their chance to change things.

THE KINGDOM DIVIDED

King Solomon died. His son Rehoboam left his palace in Jerusalem, and traveled north to the city of Shechem. Jeroboam and the leaders of Israel came to him. "We want to be loyal to you," they said, "but your father, King Solomon, made life too hard for us. If you will treat us better, we will support you."

Rehoboam asked his advisers what to do. "Jeroboam has a point," they said. "You should do as he asks and make things easier for the ordinary people." But Rehoboam rejected their advice. "If you think Solomon was cruel, there will be a lot worse to come from me!" he told the people.

This was too much! All the tribes from the north went home. And that was the end of the great kingdom which Solomon and his father, David, had built up. The only people who stayed loyal to Rehoboam were those who lived in the south, near Jerusalem. From now on, they were known as the nation of Judah.

The rest of the people had had enough. They wanted fair and just rule. They made Jeroboam their king, and they were known as the nation of Israel.

2 Kings of Israel

Jeroboam had great hopes for the new, breakaway kingdom of Israel. He wanted his people to keep God's laws as their ancestors had done.

To help them remember these laws, he built two new temples: one at Dan, in the far north, and the other at Bethel, near the border of Judah. A golden bull statue stood in each of them. These bulls were meant to represent God's throne, just as the covenant box did in Jerusalem. But the people worshiped them as if they were gods. Because of this, Jeroboam lost many of his supporters.

He died in 910 B.C. For the next thirty-five years Israel was ruled by one weak king after another.

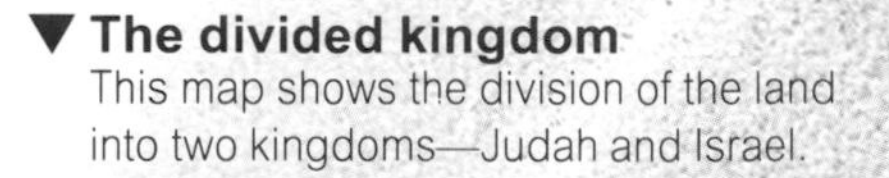

▼ The divided kingdom
This map shows the division of the land into two kingdoms—Judah and Israel.

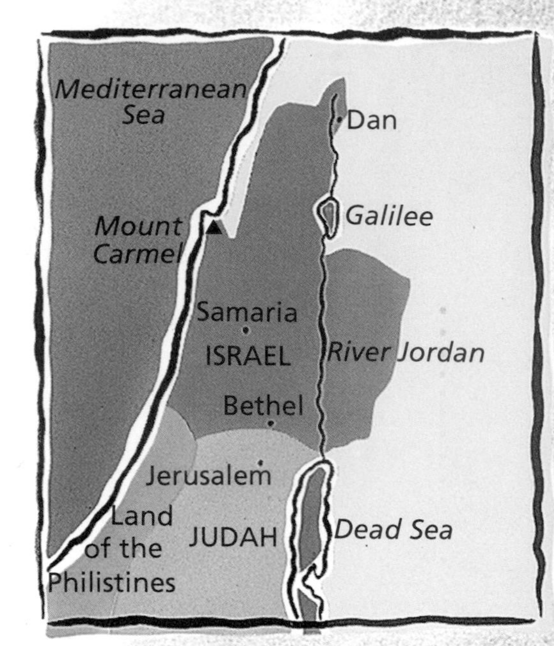

Omri builds a city

Thirty-five years after the death of Jeroboam, a man named Omri became king. He was a skillful ruler and he brought peace to the land. He even made friends with the king of Judah!

He decided to give his people something they could be proud of: a new capital city. He bought a hill and built a strong fortress town there: Samaria.

◀ The ruins of Samaria
The kings who built Israel's capital city of Samaria were rich and powerful. Even these ruins give a hint of the might of their city.

▶ God takes care of Elijah
The Bible story says that when Elijah first escaped from King Ahab's anger, he lived near a brook in the wild and ravens brought him food. Later, a widow and her son in Zarephath provided a home for him. God took care of them all, and their meager food supply never ran out.

Ahab

Omri's son Ahab became the next king in Israel. He inherited power from his father, and he wanted to keep it. But he was not greatly concerned about God. Not everyone was happy with the way things were going in Israel under his rule. One man in particular—a prophet named Elijah—was ready to speak out.

ELIJAH AND THE DROUGHT

Life was getting tough in Israel for those who tried to keep God's laws. Ahab—Israel's seventh king—married Jezebel, a princess from the city of Tyre. She worshiped the gods and goddesses of the Canaanites, and persuaded Ahab to do the same. Although he knew that many of his people wanted him to follow God's law, Ahab let Jezebel have her way. Those who spoke out for God were thrown into prison, or even killed.

One day, God sent a message to a prophet called Elijah. "Go to King Ahab and tell him I have seen all the cruel things he is doing, and that he will be punished. There will be no more rain in Israel until I say so."

Without rain, no crops would grow. Elijah knew the king would be angry. But he delivered the message all the same. Someone *had* to speak out. Worshiping false gods led to injustice and unfairness.

Elijah was right about the king being angry! But God sent him to stay in a safe place until it was time for action.

The prophets

The Bible prophets were people who spoke on behalf of God.

Sometimes prophets received messages in dramatic ways, through visions or dreams.

At other times they discovered what God was saying by studying God's laws. They all wanted their people to stay loyal to the plan for their nation that God had given to their ancestors when they escaped from slavery in Egypt.

The prophets of Israel believed there was a big difference between their nation and other nations. The stories people told about foreign gods—such as the Canaanite god Baal—showed these gods to be cruel and selfish. And indeed, the Canaanite kings were often cruel and selfish like their gods!

But that was not the Israelite way. The prophets believed that God always cared for ordinary people. That meant Israel's kings should never have favorites, or take advantage of others who were weaker.

It was the job of Israel's prophets to make sure this difference was never forgotten.

3 Elijah and the Prophets of Baal

King Ahab continued to show no respect for God. Instead, he worshiped Canaanite gods and goddesses. Many other people in the nation of Israel also believed it was important to worship these gods—the old gods of the land.

Questions about God's power

People in the ancient world worshiped many gods and goddesses. Different gods were believed to have power over different things.

Each country had its own gods, and sometimes there were different ones in each town or city.

When the people of Israel settled in the land of Canaan, they looked back to their escape from Egypt and knew that "the Lord" of whom Moses had spoken had great power in Egypt. This God had also guided them safely through the desert and certainly knew how to help them raise sheep and goats.

But did "the Lord" have power in the new land of Canaan? Did "the Lord" know how to help them grow crops? They were not at all sure.

The Canaanite god Baal

The Canaanites believed that one of their gods, Baal, controlled the storms and rain. If that was true, then it meant farmers in the land of Canaan could only grow good crops if they worshiped him.

So, when the Israelites came to the land and saw how well the Canaanite farmers did by worshiping Baal, they were tempted to do the same—just to be on the safe side.

Elijah knew that God's laws told the people of Israel to trust in "the Lord" alone. He believed that disobeying God's laws was never right, and that in the end it would lead to disaster.

But what could he do to convince the people of Israel? One day, there was a great showdown.

▲ **Baal**
This picture of Baal is based on an ancient carving from Syria.

THE FIRE BEFORE THE RAIN

There had been no rain in Israel for three years when the prophet Elijah returned to King Ahab's palace. "Look at all the trouble you've brought on our people. They're almost starving," Ahab complained.

"No," Elijah replied, "this is all your fault. If you were not worshiping Baal, none of this would have happened. Now summon the people and all the prophets of Baal to meet me on Mount Carmel."

The king set up the meeting and, when everyone was there, Elijah spoke to them.

"It's time you made up your minds," Elijah said. "You can't worship two gods at once. Let's see which is the true one. If it's 'the Lord,' then that is who you should worship. But if it's Baal, then worship him."

So they put it to the test. They built two altars—one for Elijah and one for the prophets of Baal, and a bull was butchered and placed on each.

"The god who sends fire to burn the sacrifice is the true one," Elijah declared.

The prophets of Baal prayed and cried out for hours. "Baal, hear us!" But nothing happened.

When Elijah's turn came, he poured water all over his altar, to make the sacrifice more difficult to burn. Then he prayed a simple prayer: "O Lord God of Israel, let the people see that you really are the true God."

At once, flames burned up the altar and everything on it. And all the people cried out: "The Lord is God; the Lord alone is God!"

Then Elijah turned to the king. "I hear the rain coming," he said.

In a little while the sky was covered with dark clouds, the wind began to blow and heavy rain began to fall. The long drought was ended.

▶Mount Carmel According to the Bible story, the contest between Elijah and the prophets of Baal took place on these slopes.

4 Elijah and the King

The showdown with the prophets of Baal left Elijah exhausted. He was also in great danger: Ahab's wife, Jezebel, was furious at what Elijah had done, and she wanted him dead.

Elijah was afraid, and he fled.

◄ **Mount Sinai**
At Mount Sinai, Elijah believed that he heard God speaking to him in a soft, quiet voice. What God said gave him new hope.

God speaks to Elijah

Elijah traveled many miles to escape Jezebel's anger, until he reached Mount Sinai, far to the south. This was where God's laws had first been given to Moses. Elijah hoped that by going back there he would meet God in some special way. He needed fresh hope to help him continue the struggle against those who worshiped Baal.

When he reached the mountain, Elijah felt really depressed and miserable. It seemed as if he was the only one left in the whole land who was interested in living the way God wanted. As he waited for God to speak to him, there came a furious wind that sent great rocks tumbling down the slopes. An earthquake shook the ground. Then there was a fire. But God did not speak through any of these.

It was as Elijah sat in the silence of the mountain that God spoke, a soft whisper of a voice. God reminded Elijah that there were at least 7,000 other people who were still faithful to the commandments.

Elijah knew it was right to continue the struggle. But now he must return to Ahab just once more, to give the king a chance to change his mind before it was too late.

KING AHAB AND THE VINEYARD

Next to King Ahab's palace at Jezreel there was a vineyard. It belonged to a man called Naboth.

"That vineyard would make a wonderful new garden," thought the king.

So he asked Naboth if he could buy it, or if he would agree to take another vineyard in exchange. But Naboth was firm.

"Oh no," he said. "That vineyard has always belonged to my family. When I die I want my son to have it. And God's law forbids me to sell it to someone else."

King Ahab was not pleased, though he knew Naboth was right. He was used to getting his own way. People did not say "No" to him!

He was in such a bad mood that Queen Jezebel asked him what was wrong.

"Aren't you the king?" she said, when he explained. "You shall have anything you want."

She did not tell Ahab her plan, but she had Naboth accused of treason, convicted and stoned to death—although he had done nothing to deserve it. Then she went to the king.

"Naboth is dead," she said. "You can have your new garden."

The king was in the vineyard when Elijah the prophet came to him.

"God won't let you get away with this," Elijah said. "You took Naboth's life and as a punishment you, Jezebel, and your whole family will be destroyed."

Elijah's words came true. Within three years Ahab was dead. He lost his life in a great battle at Ramoth-gilead. His son Ahaziah became king in his place. But he didn't last long either. Joram, who followed him as king, was soon overthrown as well.

The royal family of Israel, founded by Omri, came to an end—because they ignored what the prophets were saying.

5 New King–New Prophet

By the time of King Joram, people in the kingdom of Israel were fed up with the kind of leadership Ahab's sons were providing. They were eager for change.

A man named Jehu took action. He was an army officer, who seized his chance to grab power for himself. He had all the remaining members of Ahab's family cruelly assassinated. He encouraged Jezebel's enemies to throw her out of the palace window to her death.

The people felt they had good reasons for supporting Jehu.

▲ Jehu pays tribute
This is part of an Assyrian carving which shows different nations bringing tribute to the Assyrian king. An inscription says that the people in this panel bring tribute from Jehu of Israel. The gifts included a golden bowl, golden goblets, golden pitchers, silver, lead, a royal staff, and a javelin.

- ▶ **Religion.** Many were horrified by the way Ahab had encouraged the worship of Baal. Jehu promised to respect God's laws.
- ▶ **Justice and fair shares for all.** Many ordinary farmers had been exploited by rich and powerful people, and they blamed Ahab and his family for it. Jehu was not from a rich family, and he looked to be the sort of person who could set things right.
- ▶ **The safety of the nation.** Other nearby nations were becoming more powerful, especially Syria and Assyria. Ahab's sons were poor soldiers, and they had no idea how to defend their nation. But Jehu was an experienced military leader.

Years later, however, a prophet by the name of Hosea pointed out that Jehu himself disregarded God's laws, even while claiming to be serving God.

Elisha

Elijah chose a new prophet to carry on the work of reminding people about God. This was Elisha, and the Bible contains many stories about Elisha that show how God was concerned about ordinary people at this time: protecting those who had fallen on hard times from loan sharks, providing food, and making drinking water safe.

Elisha was less stern than Elijah had been, but he still called on everyone he met to worship the God of Israel.

▲ Elijah's farewell
The Bible tells a story about Elijah's farewell. It says that the waters of the River Jordan changed course to allow Elijah and Elisha to cross. On the other side, Elijah was taken up to heaven in a chariot of fire. This story is set on the banks of the River Jordan, near Jericho.

Elisha heals Naaman

Naaman was a great man in Syria. As commander of the king's army, he had everything: power, fame, money, a big house, and plenty of servants to wait on him. But he also had a terrible skin disease, for which there was no cure.

One of Naaman's servants was a young Israelite girl who had been captured in a raid.

"There is a prophet back in Israel who could heal the master," she told Naaman's wife.

So the king of Syria arranged for Naaman to go to Israel to find the prophet Elisha. When Naaman arrived at Elisha's home, he expected the prophet to come out and perform some dramatic miracle. Instead, he sent his servant to the door, with a simple message.

"Elisha says you must go and wash seven times in the River Jordan," he said, "then you will be cured."

Naaman was not impressed—especially when he saw the River Jordan.

"If all I have to do is wash, there are much cleaner rivers back home in Syria," he grumbled. "This water is dirty—and it smells."

But his servants persuaded him at least to try. So he went to the River Jordan, washed in it seven times as Elisha had said—and he was completely cured.

"Now I know that the God of Israel is the only true God," he said.

6 The Assyrians

The Assyrians became the most powerful nation in the Middle East in the centuries when Israel was ruled by kings.

Their rise to power began in 911 B.C., and within a few years both Israel and the nation's old enemy, Syria, faced the same threat: Assyria's powerful king, Shalmaneser III, was leading an army to attack them. King Ahab of Israel joined forces with Syria in a great battle at Qarqar in 853 B.C. Shalmaneser did not take control of Israel that time, but within a few years, the new king Jehu was forced to bow down to him as he brought him rich gifts (see page 5).

▼ The royal zoo
The Assyrians loved to collect unusual plants and animals from the lands they conquered. At the same time that Jehu brought his gifts to Shalmaneser, elephants, apes, and other animals were brought from Egypt—perhaps for the royal zoo.

▲ The Assyrian empire
At its most powerful, Assyria ruled most of the Near East.

The height of Assyrian power

From 824 to 744 B.C.—nearly a hundred years—Assyria was busy fighting enemies to the north. Then, with the ambitious king Tiglath-Pileser III (745–727 B.C.) to lead them, the Assyrians turned their eyes on the fertile lands to the south again. Tiglath-Pileser dealt ruthlessly with countries that refused to do as he wanted. His armies would invade and besiege the main cities, and then the king and other leading citizens would be taken away many hundreds of miles to live in exile in other parts of the Assyrian empire.

The people of Israel fell to the might of Assyria in this way (page 8) and the southern kingdom of Judah only just escaped the same fate (page 9).

◀ **Elaborate carvings**
The Assyrians were great artists. Many of their sculptures and paintings show scenes from victorious battles, or the wealth and splendor of the royal court. This scene shows King Assurbanipal and his queen relaxing in the royal garden.

▲ **The Assyrian army**
This picture shows archers and slingers. The Assyrian soldiers were a powerful and terrifying force:

. . . here they come, swiftly, quickly! None of them grow tired; none of them stumble. They never doze or sleep. Not a belt is loose; not a sandal strap is broken. Their arrows are sharp, and their bows are ready to shoot. Their horses' hoofs are as hard as flint, and their chariot wheels turn like a whirlwind.

A great library

The Assyrians were cultured people. King Assurbanipal (669–627 B.C.) collected a great library of tens of thousands of clay tablets. Much of what is known about the ancient world comes from this library.

▲ **Winged bull**
Huge winged creatures flanked many entrance ways in Assyrian palaces. Here, teams of workers transport a roughly-carved winged bull from the quarry.

The end of the empire

The Assyrian empire collapsed not long after the defeat of Israel. It was replaced by the Babylonian empire in 609 B.C.

7 Prosperity—and Disaster

For thirty years after Jehu died, Israel had several weak kings. Then Jeroboam II became king. He rebuilt the capital Samaria. People got richer, and it seemed as if Israel would again be a great nation.

▲ God's promises for new life
The prophet Hosea said that God promised to forgive the people of Israel. Then they would flourish like a vineyard, producing good fruit.

The temptations of riches

Just as in the time of Solomon and Ahab, the nation got richer by neglecting God's laws. Some were even unsure what God's laws really said. This was such a problem that the educated people in Israel who knew the stories of their nation's past recorded them—a great history of their people going back to the very beginning of time. They hoped that people would learn from their history: perhaps they would see just how far they had moved from the kind of nation God intended them to be—and then change their ways.

▲ Amos and the corn sieve
A traditional wicker sieve from Israel, used to sieve good grain from rubbish. Amos warned the people of his day that God would sift them—and not many good people would be found.

A prophet's warnings

Amos was a shepherd in the village of Tekoa, over the border in Judah. God called him to take a stern warning to Israel.

As Amos mixed with the crowds in the great religious centers of Bethel and Gilgal, he could see they thought their nation was rich because they were very religious. But Amos knew there were many poor people who were being exploited by these religious people. He brought them some harsh messages from God. Here is one of the things Amos said:

> *Stop all this noisy worship. God is not interested in hearing fine music. Instead, there should be justice and fairness flowing like a great river through the whole nation. Religion has no value at all if it does not improve people's lives. Unless you change your ways, you rich people can only expect judgment. The Assyrian armies are already on their way, and when they arrive they will shake the whole nation up like corn in a sieve—and not much will be left.*

Hosea's final plea

After Jeroboam II, none of the kings of Israel ruled for long. Israel grew weaker. Assyria was getting stronger. A prophet named Hosea pleaded with the people to turn back to God. He experienced much sadness when his wife left him, for he still loved her very much. He knew this was how God must have felt when the people followed their own ways.

"COME BACK TO ME"

The prophet Hosea was married to a girl called Gomer and he loved her very much. Together they had three children.

But Gomer was not faithful to her husband. One day, she left him and did not come back.

Hosea was heartbroken.

"I know how you are feeling," God said. "I love the people of Israel every bit as much as you love Gomer. But they no longer love me. They have gone away from me, just as Gomer has deserted you."

God had more to say:

"Don't stop loving Gomer, any more than I have stopped loving Israel. Go and find her and win her back."

So that is what he did. And he told the people of Israel how much God had always loved them—how God still loved them, even though they had worshiped the gods and goddesses of Canaan.

"You have brought suffering on yourselves," God said. "The Assyrians are coming. But I love you still. Come back to me."

Sadly, Israel ignored Hosea's words, just as they ignored Amos.

8 The End of a Kingdom

When Jeroboam II died, the kingdom of Israel was left in turmoil. There were many revolts against the people who tried to claim power, and kings were assassinated. Meanwhile, the threat from Assyria was looming ever larger.

The alliance that never was

Syria to the north, Israel, and Judah: three kingdoms, all facing the same enemy. Could they possibly get together and form an alliance, to fight the common enemy?

Syria and Israel both tried to persuade Jotham, king of Judah, to join them in resisting the Assyrians. He refused. When Jotham's son Ahaz became king in Judah, Syria and Israel declared war to try to force him to do as they wanted.

Ahaz was terrified. One of his advisers, the prophet Isaiah, told him to do nothing. But instead he invited the Assyrians to help him. They attacked the Syrian capital, Damascus, killed the Syrian king, and removed many of his people to other parts of the empire. In return for this help, Ahaz of Judah was forced to pay tribute to the Assyrian emperor, Tiglath-Pileser III.

▲ Tiglath-Pileser III
The Assyrian emperor who destroyed Israel is shown on this ancient carving.

The last days of Israel

The kings of Israel continued to suffer at the hands of the Assyrians. When a man named Pekah became king, he gave up land to the Assyrians to try to avoid being completely overrun. A rival Israelite, Hoshea, was dismayed at his weakness. He assassinated Pekah—but ended up paying tribute money to the Assyrians himself.

When the Assyrian king Tiglath-Pileser died and was replaced by a king named Shalmaneser, Hoshea thought he saw a chance. He asked the king of Egypt to help him fight off the Assyrians.

It was a stupid idea. The new Assyrian king, Shalmaneser V, decided to show who was the boss. He invaded, destroyed Israel's capital city of Samaria, and took 27,290 of its citizens to live as exiles in other countries.

By 722 B.C. the nation of Israel was finished. Amos's dreadful warning of judgment and destruction really had come true.

▼ Exiles
The people of Israel were forced into exile, traveling on foot or in carts. Any who resisted were cruelly punished by the Assyrian soldiers.

The "lost tribes"

Solomon's great kingdom consisted of twelve tribes. But ten of them had joined Jeroboam I to set up the kingdom of Israel some 200 years earlier, leaving just two tribes to form the kingdom of Judah. When the Assyrians destroyed Israel and took its people away, that was the end of these ten tribes.

No one knows for sure just where they went, or what happened to them. All that is known is that the Assyrians settled them somewhere else in their empire. Over time, their young people found husbands and wives for themselves among the people of other races in the lands where they lived. In the end, they could no longer be identified as the people of Israel.

Two prophets: Isaiah and Micah

Isaiah belonged to an upper-class family in Judah. It may even have been the royal family! He was married, and his wife was also a prophet. God called him to be a prophet just as Jotham began ruling Judah, but most of his messages were delivered during the reign of Jotham's son Ahaz and his grandson, Hezekiah.

Isaiah's messages can be found in the book of Isaiah. It is one of the longest books in the Hebrew Scriptures. Isaiah could see the kingdom of Israel was in deep trouble because its people ignored God's laws—and exactly the same thing was starting to happen in Judah as well. Although he came from a wealthy family, he didn't have much sympathy for the rich and powerful.

"

You are doomed! You make unjust laws that oppress my people. That is how you prevent the poor from having their rights and from getting justice.

The prophet Micah was a farmworker. He knew how hard life was becoming for poor people. But he saw things the same way as Isaiah, and called on everyone to sort out what was really important in their life:

God is not interested in sacrifices and empty religious rituals. True goodness is doing what's right, caring for others, and humbly trusting God.

9 Life in Judah

The kingdom of Judah fared better than Israel. There were good times, when life was calm and peaceful. People enjoyed a good standard of living.

Mistakes and warnings

However, the people of Judah made exactly the same mistakes as Israel. In the time of King Ahaz, for example, all kinds of gods and goddesses were worshiped in the temple at Jerusalem. The prophet Isaiah gave Ahaz a stern warning in God's name:

Do you think I want all these sacrifices you keep offering? I am disgusted with the smell of it all, and I hate all your special festivals for new moons and holy days. Stop all this pointless worship, and attend to the things that are really important—acting fairly, helping those who are oppressed, giving poor people their rights . . .

But Ahaz paid no attention. Trying to protect himself from Israel and Syria, he even went and asked the Assyrians for help! Isaiah told him this move would bring disaster:

You have rejected the quiet waters from the brook of Shiloah (near Jerusalem) for the flood waters of the (Assyrian) River Euphrates overflowing all its banks.

Once the kingdom of Israel had been destroyed, the border of the Assyrian empire was very near to Jerusalem itself. There seemed nothing else to do but become allies with the Assyrians—yet they were dangerous people. It was not easy for Judah's kings to know how to act wisely.

Hezekiah, the son of Ahaz, faced the worst threat of all: the attack on his fortified cities . . . including Jerusalem.

◀ **A city of Judah destroyed**
During the reign of the Assyrian king Sennacherib, the Assyrians attacked and destroyed the fortified cities of Judah. Many engraved panels showing their capture of the city of Lachish have been found. This one shows the Assyrian siege machines coming close to the walls, under a rain of firebrands hurled by the people defending the city.

THE SIEGE OF JERUSALEM

No sooner had Hezekiah become king of Judah than the Egyptians and the Philistines asked him to join them in a revolt against Assyria. The prophet Isaiah knew this would spell disaster. He took off all his clothes and walked with nothing on around the streets of Jerusalem.

"This is how you'll all end up," he said, "led away naked as prisoners of Assyria."

He got people's attention—and they took his warning seriously.

Hezekiah wanted to make the changes for the better that he could see his kingdom needed. He banned from the temple the worship of Assyrian and Canaanite gods. And he strengthened Jerusalem's fortifications against an Assyrian attack.

It was not long in coming. Seven years after they had destroyed the kingdom of Israel, the Assyrians marched into Judah. They attacked the border fortresses. Nearer and nearer they came until they were at the gates of Jerusalem itself. They had King Hezekiah and Isaiah and all the people shut up inside like birds in a cage.

King Sennacherib of Assyria sent a message to King Hezekiah.

"I will destroy your city," he said. "Don't think your God can save you—surrender now."

Hezekiah prayed a desperate prayer:

"O God, you are King above every king. Please rescue us from the Assyrians."

Isaiah stayed calm. "Don't worry. This time, God will save the city."

That night, a dreadful thing happened in the Assyrian camp. Thousands of Assyrian soldiers died. No one knew why, but the next morning the camp was full of dead bodies. The Assyrian king went home to his capital city of Nineveh. Jerusalem was left in peace.

▼ The Assyrian messenger
The Assyrian messenger ignored Hezekiah's refusal to surrender. He called to the people on the city walls, telling them to give up.

◀ Secret water supply
King Hezekiah had a long tunnel built from inside Jerusalem to a spring outside the walls. This secret water supply helped the people survive the long siege.

10 Good King Josiah

When Hezekiah died, his son Manasseh became king, and Manasseh's son Amon after that. They ignored what the prophets had said and neglected God's laws. They worshiped foreign gods in the temple built by Solomon hundreds of years earlier.

But Amon's son Josiah was different. He was brought up by foster parents, and that helped him decide for himself how to do what was right. He was a boy when he became king, but he quickly saw that it was up to him to make some big changes in his kingdom.

JOSIAH'S BIG CHANGES

When Josiah became king, the temple in Jerusalem contained all sorts of things that had nothing to do with worshiping God. Many of the objects were used to worship other gods, the gods of the Assyrians. Josiah gave orders for the temple to be repaired. Someone discovered a book of God's laws in the building. It was agreed that the king should hear them.

When Josiah heard the laws read, he was dismayed.

"It is years and years since these laws were kept," he said. "We have broken our promises to God."

What was to be done?

Josiah asked the advice of a woman called Huldah—a prophet famous for her wisdom.

"This is what God says," Huldah replied. "My people have not obeyed me. They have worshiped false gods, and broken my laws—and they will be punished. But because Josiah the king is loyal to me, I will not punish them for as long as he is alive."

God's laws were read aloud to the people, reminding them of the time when Moses led their ancestors out of Egypt. They decided to make a fresh start: both the king and the people renewed their promises to God. Josiah had the temple cleared of all the things that did not belong to the worship of God. And everyone celebrated a great Passover festival—something that had not happened in Judah for many years.

King Josiah loved God with all his heart, and while he lived, all was well in Judah.

Did you know?

When Josiah cleared out the contents of the temple in Jerusalem, he was not just spring-cleaning! Subject nations usually worshiped the gods of their overlords. That was how they showed they intended to do as they were told. The Assyrians expected altars to their gods to be placed in the temple as signs that Judah would be loyal.

For most nations this was no problem. But the Hebrew Scriptures spoke of just one God whom people should serve. The prophets told the people that ignoring this law was what had brought ruin to Israel. The people of Judah would be foolish to make the same mistake.

The end of Josiah's reign

During Josiah's reign the Assyrians' power grew weaker. There were revolts within their own homelands, and the king of Babylon grew increasingly powerful. Egypt was one of Assyria's sworn enemies, but when the king of Egypt saw Babylon getting stronger he joined forces with the Assyrians to try to stop it.

Josiah was very worried. His own kingdom lay between these two great powers. He went to battle to try to stop the Egyptians from supporting the Assyrians. In the battle, Josiah was killed.

His son Jehoahaz reigned for less than a year: the Egyptians came back to take revenge for Josiah's attempt at defeating them, and took him away to Egypt. They made another of Josiah's sons king. This was Jehoiakim.

But now the Babylonians were getting stronger all the time. Judah faced a serious threat from them.

▼ An Assyrian god
The Assyrian weather god is shown in an ancient carving clutching lightning flashes.

11 The Babylonians

Babylon was in the southern part of the land known today as Iraq. It was a fertile region, watered by the River Euphrates. The city may have been inhabited as long ago as 4000 B.C.

The cradle of civilization

Between about 3000 and 2000 B.C., the civilizations of the Sumerians and the Akkadians flourished in this area. Archaeologists have discovered many objects from this time, including the world's earliest writings and many items of fine jewelry. The people of ancient Babylon discovered many new things about astronomy, mathematics, and the calendar, and their city became the center of great learning. The Bible story of the tower of Babel is set in ancient Babylon.

▼ **A game board from ancient Babylonia**

Did you know?

One of the most famous kings of ancient Babylon was Hammurabi, who reigned from about 1792 to 1750 B.C. During his reign he made important changes to the law, and he is best known for this "law code." He also gave great encouragement to people working in the arts.

His family lost power to another nation, the Hittites, in 1595 B.C., and from then on until the collapse of the Assyrian empire, Babylon was controlled by other nations.

The new Babylonian empire

When the Assyrian empire came to power, it ruled over Babylon. Babylon still had its own kings but they were forced to do as the Assyrians told them. When Nabopolassar became king of Babylon on November 22, 626 B.C., he could see that the Assyrians were already losing control of the empire. This gave him the chance to make Babylon great again, and in no time at all, the Babylonians drove the Assyrians back toward their own city of Nineveh.

For the next 80 years, Babylon would be the most powerful nation in the whole region.

Did you know?

On the roof of the palace, Nebuchadnezzar built landscaped gardens to please his queen, who greatly missed the hills of her homeland. They are known as the hanging gardens of Babylon.

▼ The Ishtar gate
The great gateway to the city of Babylon was dedicated to the goddess Ishtar.

▼ The processional way
In this Babylonian festival, a statue of the god Marduk is taken out of the city on a boat. Such worship of idols was a problem for the people of Judah.

Nebuchadnezzar

Nabopolassar was succeeded by his son Nebuchadnezzar (605–562 B.C.). Between them they rebuilt old Babylon and constructed many new attractions. Their capital city was admired throughout their empire.

▼ A map of the Babylonian Empire

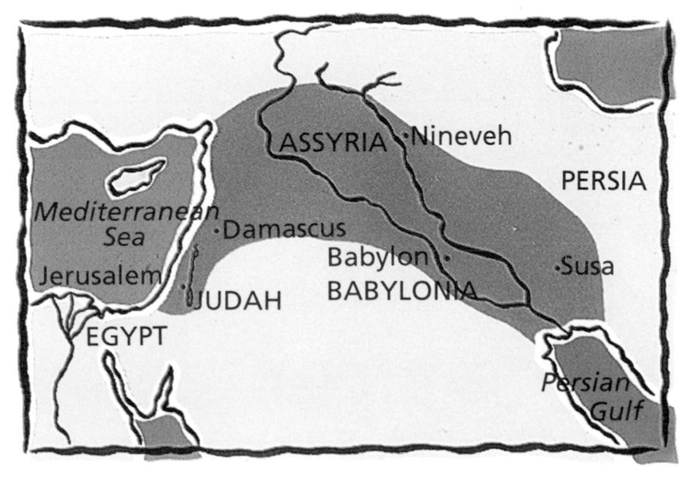

► Nebuchadnezzar's brick
Some of the bricks used to build the city of Babylon were stamped with the name of the king, Nebuchadnezzar.

12 Siege and Destruction

Jehoiakim had been made king of Judah by the Egyptians. When the Egyptians were defeated by the Babylonian armies, Jehoiakim had to switch his loyalty.

Jeremiah's warnings

A prophet named Jeremiah had repeatedly warned the rulers of Judah that disaster would come if they did not obey God's laws.

Once, Jeremiah saw a pot of water on an open fire. "God's anger is at the boiling point," he told the people. "Armies from the north will come and besiege your cities, and God will punish you."

Josiah had wanted the people to listen and change their ways. But when Jehoiakim became king, Jeremiah was beaten up and put in the stocks. Jehoiakim tossed his words of warning into a fire.

Foolishly, he rebelled against the Babylonians. At once, Nebuchadnezzar, the Babylonian emperor, marched to Jerusalem and besieged it. Before the siege had ended, Jehoiakim died, and his son Jehoiachin became king in his place.

►After Jerusalem fell
The Bible tells of people competing with wild animals for scraps of food among the ruins of Jerusalem.

Judah's last days

Jehoiachin hoped it might be possible to negotiate with the Babylonians, and so he immediately surrendered to them. Nebuchadnezzar was deeply suspicious. He had no idea whether Jehoiachin could be trusted. To be on the safe side, he marched him off into exile in Babylon, along with many of the leading politicians. He also helped himself to most of the national treasures from the temple and royal palaces.

Nebuchadnezzar made Zedekiah king of Judah. But nothing changed. Zedekiah himself tried to revolt against the Babylonians. This time, Nebuchadnezzar was furious, for he himself had given Zedekiah a position of trust and power. He came back with an even bigger army, and Jerusalem was under siege for eighteen months.

The end came. Zedekiah was captured, his family were all killed and he himself was blinded before being carried off to exile in Babylon. With him went many of the people left in Jerusalem. All the main buildings were destroyed, including the temple.

Facing up to disaster

Many centuries before, God had called the people's ancestor Abraham to leave his home in Babylonia and travel west to be the founder of a great nation. Now the nation's leaders had been taken back to Babylon as prisoners, and the beautiful city of Jerusalem—sometimes referred to as Zion—was in ruins. It was a time of great sadness for all the people. They began to wonder what had happened to all the great promises God had given them.

Our glittering gold has grown dull;
the stones of the Temple lie scattered in the streets.
Zion's young men were as precious to us as gold,
but now they are treated like common clay pots.
People who once ate the finest foods
die starving in the streets;
those raised in luxury are pawing through garbage for food...
Those who died in the war were better off than those who died later,
who starved slowly to death,
with no food to keep them alive.

The lost ark

The covenant box (sometimes called the ark of the covenant) was kept in the temple and contained God's laws. It has never been traced since the time when Solomon's temple was destroyed. Its loss was a bitter blow to the people—for it had been a symbol that God was with them.

13 Prophets of Doom and Hope

The prophet Jeremiah came from a family of priests who lived near Jerusalem. He was deeply saddened when he saw the temple destroyed by the Babylonians—the place where God should have been worshiped.

But he did not lose hope. In the end, he knew that God's promises were not about cities and buildings, but about people. He looked forward to a day when God would make new promises to the people. Their wrongdoings would be forgiven, and they would make a new start.

> *The Lord says:*
> *"My people are like sheep whose shepherds have let them get lost in the mountains . . . they have been chased and scattered by lions . . . but I will give them a new chance . . . I will forgive those people . . ."*

◀ **Enemies**
The people of Israel were scattered by their enemies as sheep are scattered by lions.

Ezekiel

Ezekiel was one of the people taken off to Babylon as a prisoner at the same time as King Jehoiachin. He became a prophet, bringing God's messages to the people.

Ezekiel's Amazing Message

Ezekiel was feeling very homesick. All his life he had looked forward to his thirtieth birthday, when he would serve in the temple as one of God's priests.

And here he was, hundreds of miles from his homeland, one of ten thousand captives taken from Judah to work on the plains of Babylonia.

Five years had passed since Ezekiel left home.

"How far away the temple is," Ezekiel thought. "How far away God seems."

A sudden gust of wind made him look up. Was that a storm coming? A strange dark cloud raced toward him. Lightning flashed. In the middle of the storm were four animals with strange faces and wings. Things like wheels were turning in every direction, and the wheels had eyes that could see in all directions.

Above the darkness, Ezekiel could see a dazzling blue—far brighter than the sky—shot with all the colors of the rainbow.

Then he heard a voice that shook the earth.

"I am sending you to warn my people. They have rebelled and turned against me. But if they mend their ways, there is still hope for them."

Then the vision was gone. Ezekiel walked trembling back to the camp. God was here—God was everywhere—after all. And God had given him a special job to do: not in the temple, but in the camp, among the exiles.

▼ Friends
Ezekiel told of God's promise to take care of the people as a shepherd takes care of sheep.

Hope for the future

Ezekiel had other things to say that brought hope to his people. He said that God would be to the people as a shepherd is to sheep.

> *I myself will be the shepherd of my sheep, and I will find them a place to rest. I, the Sovereign LORD, have spoken.*
>
> *I will look for those that are lost, bring back those that wander off, bandage those that are hurt, and heal those that are sick.*

In another vision, Ezekiel was in a valley, with old skeletons all around him. "Tell these bones to come alive again," the voice of God said. Ezekiel did so, and to his amazement that is exactly what happened. "I will breathe new life into my people, just as I did into these bones. They will go back to their own land, and this time they will be loyal to me. Tell them it's a promise—and I always keep my promises."

It gave the people new hope, and those in exile began looking for the chance to go back to their home in Jerusalem.

14 Exiles in Babylon

Life was not all bad for the exiles in Babylon. King Jehoiachin, whom Nebuchadnezzar had taken off to Jerusalem before he finally destroyed the city, was still known as "king of Judah," and he seems to have had a special role in the Babylonian court.

But many of them did not want to lose their own way of life. As the people from "Judah," they became known as "Jews," and the so-called "Jewish" customs about preparing food in a special way and keeping the sabbath as a day of rest became very important to them.

Daniel

Daniel was an upper-class teenager who was taken to live at the court of King Nebuchadnezzar. He and his three friends, Shadrach, Meshach, and Abednego, were trained to be advisers to the king.

But they were determined not to forget that they were Jewish people. Instead of eating the king's food, they chose a simple diet that was allowed by their own laws.

Nebuchadnezzar was surprised when they turned down the chance of a rich lifestyle, but Daniel and his three friends were so good at their job that the king knew there was no point in making a fuss about it.

►After the fire
According to the Bible, when King Nebuchadnezzar finally saw how God took care of the people from Judah, he said, *"Praise the God of Shadrach, Meshach, and Abednego! He sent his angel and rescued these men who serve and trust him. They disobeyed my orders and risked their lives rather than bow down and worship any god except their own."*

THE FIERY FURNACE

One day, King Nebuchadnezzar made a gold statue of one of his Babylonian gods. It was huge—over 30 meters high. And all the important people were ordered to come to the ceremony of dedication. A great orchestra was there to play special music.

"As soon as the music starts," said the king, "we will all bow down and worship the god. If you don't, then I'll have you thrown into the hottest furnace I can find."

Everyone did exactly as the king said—except for Shadrach, Meshach, and Abednego.

"The God we worship can save us from your fire. But even if we are burned, there is no way we will ever worship any other god."

Nebuchadnezzar was furious. He had his furnace stoked up, and the three friends were bound up and thrown into it. As he looked in from a distance, the king was amazed at what he saw. Not only were they walking around in the flames, but there was someone else in there with them.

"It must be a god," Nebuchadnezzar exclaimed. At once he had them come out of the fire, and to everyone's surprise not even their hair had been burned.

"Your God must be something really special," Nebuchadnezzar told them. And then he added, "No one is to say a word against the God whom these men worship."

▲ Synagogue and temple
Since early times Jews have decorated their synagogue with symbols to remind them of the temple. This synagogue mosaic from the fourth century C.E. shows a menorah—the seven-branched lampstand that was part of the temple furniture.

Did you know?

Nowadays, Jewish people all around the world worship regularly at the synagogue. Before the exile into Babylon, all worship centered on the temple Solomon had built in Jerusalem. But once that was destroyed, and the people scattered into different countries, they needed a new place of worship. A synagogue in each community where there were at least ten men became that place.

Temple worship had included animal sacrifices, and the people believed the temple was the only place where they should be offered. So in the synagogue, worship consisted of prayers, reading of the Scriptures, and sometimes a sermon explaining what the Scriptures meant.

The synagogue also served as a kind of community center for Jewish people, and was the place where children could learn about the traditions and language of their nation.

15 Longing for Home

Many of the Jews who lived in exile became quite successful in their new community. They did well in business, and some even grew quite rich.

Yet as a people the Jews never felt that they belonged in Babylon. However good life there might be, it was not the same as being back home in Judah. They still had a special affection for Jerusalem, and the hill within the city where God's temple ought to be: Mount Zion.

By the rivers of Babylon we sat down;
there we wept when we remembered Zion.
On the willows near by we hung up our harps.
Those who captured us told us to sing;
they told us to entertain them:
"Sing us a song about Zion."
How can we sing a song to the LORD in a foreign land?

▲ Captive musicians
This Assyrian engraving shows musicians being led away into captivity—just as the Jews were led away to Babylon.

New hopes

As time passed, people began to think it might be possible for them to return back home to the land of Judah.

- They thought about the things that the prophets had said.... Ezekiel had spoken of how God could breathe new life even into dead bones.... Jeremiah had looked forward to a time when God's ancient promises would really come true....
- Those who were experts in their nation's history began looking to the stories of their past. They discovered that whenever the people had truly obeyed God, then life went well for them. Could it happen again?
- The answer to that question came in a whole series of messages that are now contained in the second part of the Old Testament book of Isaiah.

"The LORD is the everlasting God; he created all the world. He never grows tired or weary.

"From the distant east and the farthest west I will bring your people home," says God. "I will tell the north to let them go and the south not to hold them back. Let my people return from distant lands, from every part of the world.

"I will show compassion to Jerusalem, to all who live in her ruins. Though her land is a desert, I will make it garden."

Hopelessness
Sometimes the exiles in Babylon felt that life was as bleak as the parched earth of the desert. But they began to hope that God would bring them new hope, as rain brings new life in the desert.

16 The Persians

In 539 B.C., the Persian king Cyrus the Great defeated the armies of Babylon. Under the rule of his son Camyses and then his successor Darius, the Persian Empire became so large that it stretched from Greece to India, and from Egypt to Mesopotamia.

The Persians did not feel the need to wrench people from their homeland, as the Assyrians and Babylonians had done. They were happy to let people stay in their own country with local leaders looking after the everyday life of their own people. All they required was loyalty to the emperor . . . and income in the form of taxes!

Good communications

Good communication was essential for a successful empire. The Persians built many roads to link different places, and there was a regular mail service between all the major cities. Letters were carried on horseback. Every 15–20 miles there were rest houses and stables, where the riders could get a fresh horse to continue their journey, or hand over their packages to another rider.

▲ **Guard**
The palace built by King Darius at Susa was decorated with pictures in the brickwork. Here is an archer in ceremonial dress—one of the Persian guard.

▼ **The Persian empire**

Speaking the same language

The Persians chose Aramaic as one of the official languages of their empire. This was similar to the Hebrew language. For centuries after the Persian empire, Aramaic remained one of the main languages spoken in Palestine—the homeland of the Jews.

◀ **Gold**
A great hoard of Persian treasure, known as the Oxus treasure, has been found. This beautiful gold ornament, similar to a large bracelet, was held aloft in royal ceremonies.

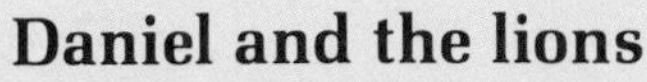

Daniel and the lions

The same Daniel who rose to a position of honor in Babylon (see page 14) appears again in a later story from the time of Persian rule. Enemies arranged to get him into trouble for worshiping his God—and had him thrown into a pit of lions. The story says that an angel kept him safe from the lions, and he was set free.

A STORY SET IN PERSIA

Haman was the chief of staff at the palace of the king of Persia. He was a proud man, and insisted everyone should kneel before him. Only one person refused: Mordecai the Jew. "My people kneel only to God," he said.

Haman was furious. He made up his mind to get rid of Mordecai and all the Jews. He went to the king with a plan.

"There are some people who refuse to obey your laws," he said. "Shall I have them punished?"

Without asking any questions, the king agreed. Haman sent letters to the governors of all the provinces, telling them to kill the Jews on a certain day.

Now Esther, the king's favorite wife, had a secret. She was Jewish—in fact, she was Mordecai's stepdaughter.

"Go to the king and plead for the lives of your people," Mordecai urged her.

It was a dangerous thing to do. If she went without being asked, the king could have her killed. But Esther bravely went. She invited both Haman and the king to dinner that night, and the party went well.

"Come back again tomorrow," she said.

On the way home, Haman saw Mordecai. Again Mordecai refused to kneel. In a great rage, Haman had a gallows built. He would have that Mordecai hanged!

The king passed a sleepless night. He sat up, reading through the palace records—and discovered that Mordecai had saved him from assassination years before.

"I must reward him," he thought.

And the next day, the king ordered Haman himself to give Mordecai royal honors in a public parade.

At dinner that night, the king thought how lovely his queen was looking.

"I will give you anything you want," he said to her.

"I and all my people are to be killed," Esther answered. "I ask for my life and the lives of my people."

The king turned pale.

"Who is responsible for this?"

"Haman," she answered.

"He has had a gallows made, ready to hang Mordecai," one of the servants added.

"Then hang him on his own gallows," said the king. And that was what they did.

Esther saved the lives of all her people that night. And the king made Mordecai his new chief of staff.

▼ Remembering Esther
Esther risked her own life when she spoke to the king. To this day, the Jews remember how Esther saved them from death. The festival is called Purim.

17 The Homecoming

Not long after he came to power, King Cyrus of Persia gave permission for all exiled people to go back to their home countries.

▲ **Cyrus's decree**
The writing on this cylinder includes the decree by the Persian emperor Cyrus allowing the Jews to return to Judah and rebuild the temple.

The pioneers

When the chance to return home became real, many of the exiles began to have doubts. It had been 40 years or more since the first Jewish exiles had arrived in Babylon, and most of them had died. Their children and grandchildren had never lived anywhere else but Babylon. They were reluctant to exchange their comfortable lifestyle there for the unknown hazards of a long journey back to Judah and the hard work of rebuilding a derelict city.

Cyrus appointed a man called Sheshbazzar to be governor of Judah. However, it was a later group led by Joshua, a priest, and Zerubbabel, who was King Jehoiachin's grandson, who really got going with the task of restoring the nation. Life was a struggle for them, and it took more than ten years to rebuild the temple. Even then, it was much poorer than Solomon's grand building had been.

▼ **Rebuilding**
Joshua and Zerubbabel watch people hard at work rebuilding Jerusalem.

Other people in the land

The land of Judah had not been empty while its people were exiled in Babylon. Nebuchadnezzar himself had left some people behind. Many of them had married people from the old nation of Israel—those remnants left behind when the Assyrians had destroyed Israel 150 years earlier. They had started a new life of their own, and a new nation, the Samarians.

At first, these people welcomed those returning from Babylon. But the Jews turned down their offer of friendship. To them, the people who had never been to Babylon were no longer real Jews, and they wanted nothing to do with them. As a result, there was hostility between the two groups for many years.

More prophets

Joshua and Zerubbabel were encouraged in their work by two prophets.

- Haggai saw people building grand homes for themselves and their families, and forgetting how important the temple of God should be. Haggai urged them to see what was really important:

If only you will put God first, then you can be sure God's promises to your nation will all come true.

- Zechariah had a similar message to encourage the people.

You will succeed not by military might, or by your own strength, but by God's spirit. Obstacles as big as mountains will disappear before you, and the temple will be the most beautiful building in the whole world.

The second temple

The second temple was finished in 515 B.C. Although it was not as grand as Solomon's temple, nor as large as the temple built much later by Herod the Great, it lasted for five hundred years—longer than either of them.

Some of the stones in this ancient wall of the temple may date back to the time of Zerubbabel.

18 A New City

The years passed. The temple had been rebuilt, but once again people had forgotton God's ancient promises to them, and they neglected to worship God there.

The city of Jerusalem was still a ruin, its walls broken down and its gates burned. A Jew who was an important official in the royal household of Persia heard all this—and he wept. His name was Nehemiah.

▲ **The splendor of Persia**
Nehemiah lived and worked in the royal household of Persia—in grand buildings similar to these at the Persian city of Persepolis. Pioneer Jerusalem seemed very poor by comparison.

Nehemiah

Nehemiah was very troubled when he heard about the neglect of Jerusalem. He went about his work with such a long face that the king noticed and asked what the matter was. When Nehemiah explained, the king offered to help in any way he could.

It was an answer to Nehemiah's prayer! He asked for permission to go to rebuild the city.

The king not only let him go, he also ordered the governors of his provinces to see that Nehemiah journeyed safely.

NEHEMIAH AND THE WALLS OF JERUSALEM

After a long journey, Nehemiah arrived in Jerusalem. He waited till it was dark. Then he rode all round the city, inspecting the walls. The next day he spoke to the priests and leaders and all the people.

"These broken-down walls are a disgrace," he said. "Let's start rebuilding! God will help."

The Jewish people set to work. But the other people in the land did not want Jerusalem to be a strong walled city again. They planned to stop the work.

At first they made fun of it. Then they planned an attack. Nehemiah prayed for God's help—and set a guard. While half the people worked, the others stood by with weapons ready.

The enemy tried new tricks. They threatened to tell the king that Nehemiah was plotting rebellion. But they could not frighten him.

With God's help, the work was finished. It had taken fifty-two days. Jerusalem was a strong walled city once again—a city to be proud of.

▼ **Rebuilding the walls**
Some of the people of Jerusalem fend off attackers while the others build. All have weapons at the ready.

Malachi and the priests

A prophet named Malachi had a special message at this time. He saw that it was not just the people but also the priests who had forgotten the worship of God:

Unless you get back to true ways of serving God, this nation has no future.

19 Rediscovering the Law

Some time after the temple was complete, a Jewish priest named Ezra arrived from Babylonia. Not only could he trace his ancestry back to Aaron, the first High Priest, but he was also a great scholar. He had given his whole life to studying God's laws, to following it himself, and to teaching the people what it meant.

Ezra calls for change

When he first arrived, Ezra was very busy organizing the temple worship and training the people who were to serve in the temple.

Then he turned his attention to something else: he saw that many people had married foreigners, who were bringing their own gods and goddesses with them. It seemed as if they were repeating all the same mistakes their ancestors had made!

Ezra read God's law to them, and demanded that anyone who really wanted to follow the law should leave their foreign wives or husbands.

Many did as Ezra suggested.

Sharing God's love

Not everyone was happy about Jews keeping themselves totally separate from other races. The story of Jonah was a great favorite with people who understood God's promises in a different way from Ezra and other hard-liners.

From the story, it is clear that Jonah thought his own people were special to God. Their history taught them so. But that did not mean God loved no one else. This was a hard lesson for the people of Ezra's day to learn. In fact, their unwillingness to share God's love with others was to store up a lot of trouble for them in the future.

▶Runaway
Jonah boarded a ship bound for Spain—as far from Nineveh as he could get!

THE STORY OF JONAH

Jonah was a prophet. One day, God spoke to him and gave him a special message.

"Go to Nineveh, where the Assyrians live, and tell them I know all about their cruel deeds. Warn them that in forty days I will destroy their city."

The Assyrians were enemies. Jonah would have been delighted to see them destroyed. But a worrying thought came to him:

"God is loving. What if the people of Nineveh get a second chance? I would look stupid then."

So he set off—but took a ship going in the opposite direction from Nineveh.

A great storm blew up.

"Ask your God to save us," the captain said to Jonah. Jonah knew he couldn't do that. He was disobeying God by being there in the first place.

"I think I'm the cause of the storm," he said. "Throw me over the side, then the sea will be calm."

In the water, Jonah was terrified. But a big fish swallowed him whole, kept him safe for three days, and then threw him up on a beach.

This time Jonah went straight to Nineveh. And it happened exactly as he'd feared. The people changed their ways, and God gave them a second chance.

Jonah was really angry. As he sat fuming with rage in the sun's heat, a plant grew and gave him some shade. But it disappeared as fast as it had grown.

"I liked that plant," he said. "I'm really sorry it's shriveled up."

"Well," said God, "if you're sorry for a plant, you may be able to see why I am concerned for the people of Nineveh, even though they're not Jews."

20 Understanding God's Promises

God had made many wonderful promises to the kings who belonged to David's family. But the history of the nation since his time had been a disappointment. Most of the kings had seemed more interested in pleasing themselves than in keeping God's law. As a result, the nation got into more and more difficulties. It had almost been destroyed.

The promise of a king

Over the years, the prophets began to see that only a new kind of king would change things: one who would truly serve God, who would never disregard God's laws, who would be a good example to the people.

There seemed little chance of an ordinary person ever being like that. If such a king was to come, then God would have to send him.

The special king God might send was spoken of as the *Messiah*—a Hebrew word meaning "the Lord's anointed one."

Words from Isaiah

Isaiah spoke of a golden age when the Messiah would come and all the world's wrongs would be put right.

"*Wolves and sheep will live together in peace,*
and leopards will lie down with young goats.
Calves and lion cubs will feed together,
and little children will take care of them.
Cows and bears will eat together,
and their calves and cubs will lie down in peace.
Lions will eat straw as cattle do....
The land will be as full of knowledge of the LORD
as the seas are full of water.

Hardship and defeat

When Joshua and Zerubbabel rebuilt the temple, the prophet Zechariah wondered if the age of the Messiah was about to dawn.

But if anything, times grew harder. The Persian empire lasted for just over 200 years, to be followed by the Greek empire founded by Alexander the Great, which was fully established by 323 B.C.

The Greeks thought their culture was far better than any other, and made all their people learn about it. This was completely alien to the Jews.

Worse was to come. In 175 B.C., Antiochus IV became ruler of Palestine. He was very cruel to any Jews who would not follow the Greek customs. His cruelty led to a Jewish revolt. But although the rebels did establish a line of Jewish kings, within a short time they were forced to take their orders from the Romans, who established their empire.

▲ **Alexander the Great**
This is the Greek leader who built up a huge empire and ruled over the Jewish people.

◀ **Greek gods**
The Jews resisted worshiping the gods of their conquerors. This carving from the Parthenon in Athens depicts three Greek gods: Iris, Hera, and Zeus.

Hope

Where was God in the middle of all this hardship? The visions contained in the book of Daniel gave hope:

> *I saw what looked like a human being approaching me, surrounded by clouds. He went to the one who had been living forever and was given authority, honor, and royal power, so that the people of all nations, races, and languages would serve him. His authority would last forever, and his kingdom would never end.*

No one really knew what these promises meant. But from that time on, more and more people were expecting God's Messiah to come to the earth.

▲ **Ezekiel's dream**
Years after Isaiah, Ezekiel dreamed of a great stream of peace and goodness flowing from Jerusalem into all the surrounding countries.

Just as plants flourish by a stream, so Ezekiel believed, God's blessings would stream from Jerusalem and bring life and healing to all the nations.

Finding Out More

If you want to know more about what you've read in *Kingdoms and Empires*, you can look up the stories in the Bible.

The usual shorthand method has been used to refer to Bible passages. Each Bible book is split into chapters and verses. Take **1 Kings 4:20–25**, for example. This refers to 1 Kings; chapter 4; verses 20–25.

1 Solomon's Kingdom

1 Kings 4:20-25; 6:1–38	**Solomon's kingdom**
1 Kings 9:15–22	**Riches and poverty**
Deuteronomy 26:5–9; Joshua 13:8—19:51	**Solomon's wrong turn**
1 Kings 12:1–20	**The kingdom divided**

2 Kings of Israel

1 Kings 12:25–30	**Kings of Israel**
1 Kings 16:23–24	**Omri builds a city**
1 Kings 16:29–33	**Ahab**
1 Kings 17:1–16	**Elijah and the drought**
2 Kings 22:3–20; Isaiah 6:8; Ezekiel 1:1-28; Amos 7:10—8:6	**The prophets**

3 Elijah and the Prophets of Baal

Numbers 13:1—14:25	**Questions about God's power**
Judges 2:11–13	**The Canaanite god Baal**
1 Kings 18:17–46	**The fire before the rain**

4 Elijah and the King

1 Kings 19:1–18	**God speaks to Elijah**
1 Kings 21:1–28; 22:29–37; 2 Kings 1:16–17; 9:14–26	**King Ahab and the vineyard**

5 New King—New Prophet

2 Kings 9:1–13, 30–37	**New king—new prophet**
2 Kings 5:1–15	**Elisha heals Naaman**

6 The Assyrians

2 Kings 15:29; 18:13—19:37	**The height of Assyrian power**
Isaiah 5:26-29	**The Assyrian army**

7 Prosperity—and Disaster

Amos 7:12–15	**A prophet's warnings**
Hosea 14:1–8	**Hosea's final plea**
Hosea 1:2–8; 2:2–6; 3:1–5; 11:1–7	**"Come back to me"**

8 The End of a Kingdom

2 Kings 16:5–9; Isaiah 7:2–9	**The alliance that never was**
2 Kings 15:27–30; 17:1–6	**The last days of Israel**
Isaiah 6:1–8; 8:3; 10:1–2; Micah 6:6–8	**Two prophets: Isaiah and Micah**

9 Life in Judah

Isaiah 1:12-17; 8:5–7	**Mistakes and warnings**
2 Kings 18:4; 19:8–36; 2 Chronicles 29:3—31:10; 32:1–8; Isaiah 20:1–6	**The siege of Jerusalem**